PORT PUERTO
TRAKL TRAKL

JAIME LUIS HUENÚN

TRANSLATED BY
DANIEL BORZUTZKY

ACTION BOOKS / NOTRE DAME IN / 2007

ACTION BOOKS

Joyelle McSweeney & Johannes Göransson, EDITORS
Jesper Göransson, ART DIRECTOR
Eli Queen, ART DIRECTOR
Kristina Sigler, ASSISTANT EDITOR
John Dermot Woods, WEB EDITOR AND DESIGNER

ACTION BOOKS
Department of English
University of Notre Dame
356 O'Shaughnessy Hall
Notre Dame, IN
46556-5639

WWW.ACTIONBOOKS.ORG

ISBN: 0-9799755-0-6
ISBN13: 978-0-9799755-0-9

Library of Congress Control
Number: 2007937570

First Edition

Thank you to the editors of the following journals for originally publishing some of these translations: *Action, Yes*; *Circumference*; *Fascicle*; and *Mandorla*.

Thank you to the Poetry Society of America for including "I returned to Port Trakl through the worst" as part of its Poetry in Motion program. This poem appeared on posters that were hung on public buses in Los Angeles.

ACTION BOOKS is deeply grateful to LOM Ediciones for permission to reprint *Puerto Trakl*.

ACTION BOOKS gratefully aknowledges the generosity of the University of Notre Dame in supporting our mission as a press.

CONTENTS

TRANSLATOR'S INTRODUCTION

From an outsider's perspective, the thought of a Mapuche poet from Southern Chile writing in the shadow of the great and tragic Austrian writer Georg Trakl, who killed himself at the age of 27, seems, if not odd, then at least notable for its inter-cultural mélange and its implications about globalization and poetry. But perhaps the question of why a poet from the "deep south" would turn to central Europe for inspiration is in itself problematic, assuming as it does a false provincialism. Huenún, in an article in the Chilean newspaper *El Mercurio*, anticipates the question, and his response offers a poignant view of his process:

> The emergence of an ethnic poetry has generated a series of extra-literary expectations, one of which seems to suggest that a writer of indigenous origins can only sing about the natural world, his ancestors, his gods and mythologies. And it's all the better if he does this in his native language. I try, simply, not to deceive; that is, I try to maintain a certain coherence between my origins, my upbringing and my literary interests and obsessions. In this sense, I think that a poet of indigenous origins raised in an urban Chilean school, as is my case, does not need to...defend his ethnic condition by writing bad ethnic poetry.[1]

In short, *Port Trakl*, written in what Huenún calls an "ascetic and neutral Spanish" is the non-didactic tale of an imaginary journey, and its protagonist is aware of the imaginary nature of this journey. The aimless wandering, the isolation, the drinking, the nostalgia, the painful self-reflection, the family and friends who are sacrificed in order to allow for the imaginary: here, amid the ruins of Port Trakl, we can't help but ponder the value of poetry in relation to the real. Ultimately, poetry could not rescue Trakl the writer from the horror and violence of the world, and so as our speaker traverses the autonomous port where the only cultural references are literary, he encounters stowaways who have "lost their language," and priests who declare that they live in a "homeland of silence."

In a Chilean context, the isolation and abandonment of Port Trakl and its residents certainly evoke the isolation and abandonment of the indigenous communities in the south. Given Huenún's conscious decision to write outside of the expectations of ethnicity, would he reject this observation? On the contrary, I think he would embrace it, and find solace in the idea that one does not need to use the language of home to evoke the social and political realities of home.

Huenún has spoken of *Port Trakl* as a representative metaphor for the way in which countries like Chile sell their souls to enter the first world, which results in, among other things, an even further abandonment of indigenous peoples[2]. And indeed, *Port Trakl* is a world whose characters do not know which world they belong to, and which world they want to belong to; and as they attempt to depart one state of exile and enter into another, we get the sense that they will always be caught between worlds: between the real and the imaginary, between speech and silence, between poetry and the impossibility of hope.

DANIEL BORZUTZKY
CHICAGO, 2007

1. This is my translation of an article by Elizabeth Neira entitled: "Jaime Huenún: Busco una coherencia entre mi origen y mi obsesión escritural." *El Mercurio*, February 22, 2002.

2. "Huenún: poesia para recuperar la memoria," an interview with Jaime Luis Huenún in *BBC Mundo*, June 12, 2004.

vii

PORT TRAKL

Bajé a Puerto Trakl entre neblinas.
Buscaba el bar de la buena suerte para charlar sobre la travesía.
Pero todos miraban la estrella polar en sus copas,
mudos como el mar frente a una isla desierta.
Salí a vagar por las calles con faroles rojos.
Las mujeres se ofrecían sin afecto, fragrantes y cansadas.
"A Puerto Trakl los poetas vienan a morir", me dijeron
sonriendo en todos los idomas del mundo.
Yo les dejé poemas que pensaba llevar a mi tumba
como prueba de mi paso por la tierra.

I got off in the fog of Port Trakl,
searching for the bar of good fortune to chat about my trip.
But everyone stared at the polar stars in their drinks,
silent like the sea off a desert island.
I went out to roam the red-lit streets.
Perfumed and bored women, selling their tired bodies.
"In Port Trakl poets come to die," they said,
smiling in all the languages of the world.
I gave them poems I planned to take to my grave
as proof of my time on Earth.

"Y si vienes a morir a Puerto Trakl,
no bebas de mi vino", dijo el tabernero.

Este bar no es la morgue de los ángeles
ni el cementerio de los fantasiosos.
Muchos hombres han cruzado el océano
por un jarro de cerveza, por una copa
de ginebra caliente.
Nadie aquí tiene patria ahora y navegar
cansa más que la nostalgia y el amor.
Eschucha, sólo eschucha el estruendo del oleaje,
mientras el mirlo clama
entre las ramas y el viento.

"And if you come to die in Port Trakl,"
said the bartender, "Do not drink my wine."

This bar is no morgue for angels,
no cemetery for dreamers.
Many men have crossed the ocean
for a pitcher of beer, for a shot
of warm gin.
Everyone here is an exile and to sail
is worse than nostalgia or love.
Listen, just listen, to the crash of the waves,
as the blackbird cries
between branches and wind.

"Aparta el mal de tu vida", decía el capellán
en el servicio del zarpe.
Los pelícanos cubrían el muelle
y hasta el puerto llegaba el resonar de las maniobras.
"Pobres ustedes", advertía el reverendo, pero nadie
comulgaba con sus dichos.
La soledad nos había curado para siempre
de todo temor
y de cualquier destino.

"Clear the evil from your life," said the chaplain
at the embarkation ceremony.
Pelicans covered the pier
and from afar one could hear the echo of the maneuvers.
"You are poor, poor" warned the reverend, but no one
took communion with his words.
Solitude had forever cured us
of all fear
and from any destiny.

Como una manera triste de predicir
miro el paso de las nubes sobre el puerto.
Sé que mi suerte no está
en ninguno de esos nimbos que regrasan al mar
movidos apenas por el viento de la literatura.
"Profetizar me asquea" podría decir
y, sin embargo, allá va mi vida,
sobrepasada por pájaros que llevan
todo el tiempo del mundo entre sus alas.

I watch the clouds drift over port
a sad forecast for the future.
Weakly pushed by the winds of literature
the clouds return to sea,
I know they are not my destiny.
"Prophecies disgust me," I say.
Still, I see my life,
beneath the birds who carry in their wings
all the time in the world.

Atravieso este bosque de abetos tormentosos.
Las estrellas caen endulzando
los lejanos abedules.
Silenciosa, una mujer aparece en la niebla
y alumbra mi camino su lámpara sin luz.

I cross this forest of tortured firs.
Falling stars sweeten
distant birch.
Silently, a woman appears in the mist
and illuminates my path.
Her lantern has no light.

Fumando en el muelle desierto
recuerdo a mis hijos,
apenas alumbrados por el sol de este anillo.
Mi paternidad se ha ido a pique;
el mercado está desierto frente a mi.
Un corazón apátrida late en esta fuga
hacia la isla prometida.
El amor ha abierto una oscura puerta
por donde paso
                    inclinándome.

Smoking on the deserted wharf
I remember my children,
barely illuminated by the sun inside this ring.
My fatherhood has gone to ruin;
I see the deserted market.
A homeless heart pounds on this voyage
to the sacred island.
Love has opened a dark door
through which I walk
                    bending.

Volví a Puerto Trakl por los peores
caminos del océano.
La única carga eran mis ojos
agotados por la sal de la tormenta.
"Capitán", me decía el timonel,
"vamos a la deriva".
Contesté que no, que íbamos derecho
al nublado puerto de mi corazón.

I returned to Port Trakl through the worst
paths in the ocean.
Weakened by salt from the storm, my eyes
were my only cargo.
"Captain," called the helmsman,
"We are drifting."
I said no, we are heading straight
for the cloudy port of my heart.

Bebimos el vodka de madame "Su"
en el hotel Melancolía.
Nos habló de sus novios,
su vejez,
y de unos gatos perdidos en el puerto.
La noche llegó desde un poema de Trakl
que ella guardaba en la memoria.
Alzamos nuestras copas y, sin prisa,
cada cual volvió a su propia
y cotidiana decadencia.

We drank Madame "Su's" vodka
in the Hotel Melancholia.
She spoke of her boyfriends,
her old age,
of some cats lost in the port.
Night fell through a poem by Trakl
stored in her memory.
We lifted our glasses and, slowly,
we each returned
to our own quotidian decadency.

Sabemos que una estrella moribunda
no se siente ni en el cielo ni en la noche —dice ella—.
Un trago más o un trago menos
no hará ninguna diferencia —dice él—.
Mejor será escuchar viejas canciones
en gramófonos enmohecidos por la nostalgia —pide ella—.
Sí, mejor será escuchar sus tontas letras
junto a parroquianos alcohólicos,
infames ye felices —dice él.

We know that a dying star
sits neither in the sky nor in the night—she says.
One drink more or one drink less
it makes no difference—he says.
Wouldn't it better to listen to old songs
on gramophones molding with nostalgia—she asks.
Yes, it would be better to listen to your silly lyrics
with these wicked and happy
bar-drunks, he says.

Todo amor cuenta las horas de su fin,
tal como el río resbala sobre peces y piedras
que cambian de corriente,
de nido y soledad.

Al pie de esta canción
mis días levantan sus pequeñas ruinas:
un pálido arco iris dando sombra a mi sangre,
las palabras que van a dar al río
de una poesía inútil,
las huellas que dejan mis pies
sobre la luz del agua.
Faroles a lo lejos
cobijan mi destino: un bar de vagabundos
donde todo fin comienza
como un sueño imposible de recordar.

Love always counts the hours to its end
like a river gliding over fish and stones
a change of current,
of nest and solitude.

At the foot of this song
my days raise their little ruins:
a pale rainbow shadows my blood,
the words of a useless poetry will give the river
the prints my feet leave
on the water's reflection.
Distant lights
harbor my destination: a bar for wanderers
where everything ends
like a dream impossible to remember

Dices que no puedes dejar de recorrer los bares
junto al mar de la mañana,
que los cuerpos llegan hasta ti
con la violencia de los puertos siempre vendidos
al peor postor.
En verdad llorarás en vano
y tu sed sólo será la vanidad de los árboles
que en la colina creen vencer el turbio cielo de la noche.
El silencio mientras tanto, hará lo suyo
a esos poemas quemándose apacibles
en los desbordados ceniceros de tu vida.

You say you can't stop going to the bars
along the morning shore,
that the bodies reach you
with that port violence always sold
to the lowest bidder.
In truth you'll cry in vain.
Your thirst will be but the vanity of the trees
on the hill that have conquered the turbulent night sky.
Meanwhile, the silence will do what it can
to those poems sweetly burning
in the overflowing ashtrays of your life.

Vi las flores morir en el mar
quemadas con la sal del horizonte.
Rosas de puerto lanzadas por una mujer
al oleaje furioso.

I saw flowers die in the sea
burnt from salt on the horizon.
A woman threw roses from the port
into the furious waves.

Una mujer escrita en la arena,
soñada por torvos marineros desaparecidos.
La longitud de su pelo alcanza
los oscuros ojos de los peces yacentes.
El musgo de su sombra cubre
las roídas murallas de los astilleros.
"La felicidad es una sombra", dice
mientras la tormenta imaginaria inunda
los quebrados ventanales del puerto.

A woman written in the sand,
the unhappy dreams of disappeared sailors.
The length of her hair reaches
the dark eyes of sleeping fish.
The moss of her shadow covers
the eroding walls of the dockyard.
"Happiness is a shadow," she says
as the imaginary storm floods in through
the port's broken windows.

Creí que pronto arribaría el barco
de la salvación.
En tanto esperaba me hundí en las cantinas
y en trabajos de puerto.
Pasaron los años, los pleitos, las mujeres
y ni sombra ni noticias del imaginado navío.
Aprendí a tolerar el paso de otros buques
contemplando en el muelle las maniobras de zarpe.
La vejez —mi horizonte— sepultó esa eperanza
perdida como un naúfrago en la turbia
mezquindad de los mares.

I thought the ship would arrive soon
from salvation.
To pass the time I submerged myself in cantinas
and in the work of ports.
Years passed, arguments, women
with no shadow nor news of the imaginary ship.
By studying from the pier their maneuverings of departure
I learned to tolerate the passing of other vessels.
Old age—my horizon—hid my hope
lost like a castaway in the ocean's
turbulent poverty.

Flores trajimos al cementerio marino,
poesía, whisky y otras vituallas.
Navegamos aquí la muerte vespertina
de quienes bajo tierra aún ansían
hacerse al azote de las rutas del mar.

We brought flowers to the ocean cemetery,
poetry, whiskey and other necessities.
We sailed the vespertine death
of those underground who wish
to conquer the paths of the ocean.

"Perdí mi idioma en la costa
ceniza de Trakl", dijo finalmente el polizón.
Encorvado entre tambores de petróleo farfullaba
el yiddish de los malecones y los bares.
"Denle restos de ropa y de comida" —ordenó, contrariado, el capitán.
"El destino de mi nave no lo cambia
un demente agonizando en sus bodegas" —sentenció.

"I lost my language on the ashen
coast of Trakl," the stowaway finally said.
Crouched between oil drums sputtering
the Yiddish of ports and bars.
"Give him scraps of food and clothes," the captain ordered, annoyed.
"My ship's course will not be changed
by a madman dying in our hold,"—he swore.

¿Qué harán a estas horas mis amigos de coñac y de anís?
No los veo todavía en este bar que llamo "Sic transit gloria mundi".
La estrella polar los guiará a sus fondeaderos de origen, cansados
y tristes, con carpetas llenas de poemas sin publicar.
Así vuelven las empleaditas al Sur Profundo,
con un hijo natural pegado al pezón de un puerto
del que jamás podrá partir.

What are they doing now, my friends who drink cognac and anise?
I haven't yet seen them in this bar I call "Sic transit gloria mundi."
The polar stars will guide them, tired and sad,
and with folders full of unpublished poems, to where they first anchored.
This is how the servants return to the Deep South,
with a native son stuck to the nipple of
a port he cannot leave.

"Capitan Melville, capitán Melville"
oí llamar, de pronto, a mis espaldas.
Mi nombre, por cierto, no es aquel
y me volví para decirlo.
"Huya del puerto, capitán —pidió la sombra—
su tripulación lo persigue" —aseguró.
Sus palabras me calaron los huesos
en mitad de una calleja
cerrada desde siempre a la luz del amanecer.

"Captain Melville, Captain Melville,"
I suddenly heard behind my back.
This, to be sure, is not my name
and I turned around to say so.
"Flee the port, captain—the shadow demanded—
your crew is after you,"—he warned.
These words pierced my bones
in the middle of this little street
cut off from the morning sun.

"La crueldad es una estación sin término",
escribió en la sucia bitácora mercante.
Entre brindis y juramentos
anotaba los dictados de su corazón.
Arrancaba después esas ficciones
y las dejaba morir en las acequias
anegadas por los desperdicios
y la lluvia.

"Cruelty is an infinite season,"
he inscribed on the dirty merchant binnacle.
Between toasts and curses
he recorded the dictums of his heart.
He then plucked out the fictions
and left them to die in the canals
that overflowed with trash
and rain.

Como un cantante de ferias y cantinas
repitiendo siempre las mismas canciones,
declamo poemas al océano.
El oleaje apaga el rumor de mi voz
y la espuma salpica estos papeles
como un escupitajo de las rocas y del agua
a mi vanidad.
Entonces imito el gesto del cantante
cuando extiende la guitara al público y le dice:
"no quiero aplausos, sólo monedas,
no quiero aplausos, sólo monedas".

Like a singer at markets and cantinas
forever repeating the same songs,
I recite my poems to the ocean.
The waves muffle the murmur of my voice
and the sea foam splashes these pages
like a wad of spit from the water and rocks
at my vanity.
Thus I imitate the singer's gesture
when I point my guitar at the audience and say:
"no applause, just coins,
no applause, just coins."

"Ahora mi patria es silencio", murmuraba el presbítero
entrando en la ancha nave de la iglesia derrumbada.
Sentado a orillas del vitral
miró su grey —polvo, arenisca—
golpeada sin piedad
por los vientos portulanos.

"Now my homeland is silence," whispered the priest
as he entered the wide nave of the dilapidated church.
Sitting near the vitreau
I see the flock—dust, sandstone—
pounded mercilessly
by the port winds.

La frontera del puerto está en tus ojos:
el horizonte y el sol
                    en una botella vacía.

The port's border is in your eyes:
the horizon and the sun

in an empty bottle.

Viejo es el puerto y no puedo aguardar
a que otra mañana me cierre el horizonte.
Bares y callejones muy poco me deben
y jamás mi mirada ha sido infinita.
La muerte y el tiempo son aquí extranjeros;
como el cambiante oleaje, nunca dejan huella.
Otra tierra ha de hallarse mejor que esta colina,
mejor que esta bahía donde muere la luz.
Otra tierra ha de hallarse donde el pan sepa a pan
y no a sudor de hombres sin patria y

                              sin destino.

54

Old is the port and I can not wait
for another morning to block the horizon.
Bars and alleyways owe me little
and my gaze has never been infinite.
Here death and time are strangers;
like fleeting waves, they never leave a print.
There is a land better than this hill,
better than this bay where light comes to die.
There is a land where the bread tastes like bread
and not like the sweat of exiled men

                                        with no destiny.

Ninguna mano despide tus ojos,
ninguna piel aguarda tu regreso.
Tu nombre, lo sabes, es una moneda
tirada con furia a los sitios eriazos.
Recuerdas la nieve cayendo a los pinos,
ahora que deambulas al garete por un puerto
nublado y solitario, tenebroso y

                              ficticio.

No hand waves goodbye to your eyes,
no skin awaits your return.
Your name, you know, is a coin
wildly tossed to savage lands.
Remember snow falling on pines
now that you aimlessly drift through
a foggy and solitary, gloomy and fictitious
                                        port.

Ebrio me despide Puerto Trakl
con el alba mojando mi cabeza.
Sin dinero, sin amigos y sin reputación
vuelvo a mis antiguos días.
La pequeña manana abre sus puertas.
Los tugurios donde beben poetas y pescadores
quedan para siempre atrás.

Drunk Port Trakl says goodbye to me
its dawn wetting my head.
With no money, no friends, no reputation
I return to my old life.
A tiny tomorrow opens its doors.
The haunts where poets and fisherman drink
forever belong to the past.

JAIME LUIS HUENÚN, a member of the Mapuche nation, grew up in the city of Osorno in Southern Chile and lives in Santiago. His books include *Ceremonias* (University of Santiago Publishing House), and *Puerto Trakl* (LOM Ediciones, 2001), and he won the Pablo Neruda National Poetry Prize in 2003. Huenún was also the recipient of a 2005 Latin American Guggenheim Fellowship. He is the editor of important anthologies of contemporary Mapuche writing, including *20 poetas mapuches contemporaneas* (Lom Ediciones), and *La Memoria Iluminada* (Centro Editor de la Diputación de Malaga). He was a featured poet in *UL: Four Mapuche Poets, An Anthology* (Latin American Literary Review Press, 1998); and he edits *Ulmapu*, a magazine of contemporary indigenous art and literature.

DANIEL BORZUTZKY is the author of *Arbitrary Tales* (Triple Press, 2005) and *The Ecstasy of Capitulation* (Blaze Vox, 2007). He lives in Chicago.

ACTION BOOKS CATALOG

2007 / 2008 ACTION BOOKS TITLES

WHIM MAN MAMMON
by Abraham Smith
ISBN 0-9765692-8-0
ISBN13: 978-0-9765692-8-2

THAUMATROPE
by Brent Hendricks
illustrations by
Lisa Hargon Smith
ISBN: 0-9765692-9-9
ISBN13: 978-0-9765692-9-9

PORT TRAKL
by Jaime Luis Huenún
translated by
Daniel Borzutzky
ISBN: 0-9799755-0-6
ISBN13: 978-0-9799755-0-9

MOMMY MUST BE
A FOUNTAIN OF FEATHERS
by Kim Hyesoon
translated by Don Mee Choi
ISBN: 0-9799755-1-4
ISBN13: 978-0-9799755-1-6

2006 ACTION BOOKS TITLES

YOU ARE A LITTLE BIT
HAPPIER THAN I AM
by Tao Lin
Winner of the 2005
December Prize
ISBN: 0-9765692-3-X
ISBN13: 978-0-9765692-3-7

YOU GO THE WORDS
by Gunnar Björling
translated by
Frederik Hertzberg
Scandinavian Series #2
ISBN: 0-9765692-5-6
ISBN13: 978-0-9765692-5-1

THE EDGE OF EUROPE
by Pentti Saarikoski
translated by Anselm Hollo
Scandinavian Series #3
ISBN: 0-9765692-6-4
ISBN13: 978-0-9765692-6-8

LOBO DE LABIO
by Laura Solórzano
translated by Jen Hofer
ISBN: 0-9765692-7-2
ISBN13: 978-0-9765692-7-5

2005 ACTION BOOKS TITLES

THE HOUNDS OF NO
by **Lara Glenum**
ISBN:0-97656592-1-3

MY KAFKA CENTURY
by **Arielle Greenberg**
ISBN:0-97656592-2-1

REMAINLAND: SELECTED
POEMS OF AASE BERG
by **Aase Berg**
translated by
Johannes Göransson
Scandinavian Series #1
ISBN:0-97656592-0-5